((((((((((**O HUMAN MICROPHONE**))))))))))

1913 Press
www.1913press.org
1913press@gmail.com

1913 is a not-for-profit collective.
Contributions to 1913 Press may be tax-deductible.

Manufactured in the oldest country in the world,
The United States of America.

Many thanks to all the artists, from this century and the last,
who made this project possible.

Founder & Editrice: Sandra Doller
Vice-Editor & Designer: Ben Doller

$13.00
ISBN: 978-0-9840297-7-8

Scott McFarland is the Executive Vice President of UIC United Faculty (AFT/IFT/AAUP).
He lives in Chicago.

((((((((((**O HUMAN MICROPHONE**))))))))))

(((((((((((**SCOTT MCFARLAND**)))))))))))

TO LAURIE JO REYNOLDS

CONTENTS

((((((((((O HUMAN MICROPHONE))))))))))

Klaatu barada nikto. Please repeat that.

))))))))))))))

We Lift Our Lamp Beside the Golden Door.
We Lift Our Lamp Beside the Golden Door.
We Are America.
We Are America.
We Are the New Colossus.
We Are the New Colossus.
Our Flame Beacons the Tired and Poor.
Our Flame Beacons the Tired and Poor.
Choose Freedom.
Choose Freedom.
Challenge Everything.
Challenge Everything.
Life's Good.
Life's Good.
Play More.
Play More.
We Know What We're Doing.
We Know What We're Doing.
The Way Life Should Be.
The Way Life Should Be.
You're In Good Hands.
You're In Good Hands.
You're the Boss.
You're the Boss.
Be Fearless.
Be Fearless.
Live Richly and Live Longer.
Live Richly and Live Longer.
You're Lovin' It.
You're Lovin' It.
Thousands of Possibilities.
Thousands of Possibilities.
We Don't Bother You.
We Don't Bother You.
See What the Future Has In Store.
See What the Future Has In Store.
We Get It.
We Get It.
We're Businessmen.
We're Businessmen.
We're Serious.
We're Serious.
Have It Your Way.
Have It Your Way.

Ideas Ahead.

Ideas Ahead.

The Way Things Are.

The Way Things Are.

You Can't Stand Your Own Mind—We Can.

You Can't Stand Your Own Mind—We Can.

We're America. Yearn to Be Free.

We're America. Yearn to Be Free.

You'll Never Get Sick of Our Insane Demands.

You'll Never Get Sick of Our Insane Demands.

We Welcome the World.

We Welcome the World.

We Won't Bother You.

We Won't Bother You.

The New Colossus Is US.

The New Colossus Is US.

Our Libraries Are Free of Tears.

Our Libraries Are Free of Tears.

))))))))))))))))

In the Seventies you were all about *Getting It Together*.
In the Seventies you were all about *Getting It Together*.
Today what you care about is *Getting It*.
Today what you care about is *Getting It*.
But you don't get it. You can't.
But you don't get it. You can't.
You're in what we call the reality-based community.
You're in what we call the reality-based community.
You believe solutions emerge from your judicious study of discernible reality
You believe solutions emerge from your judicious study of discernible reality
but that's not the way the world really works anymore.
but that's not the way the world really works anymore.
The days of just skating by and hoping for big turnouts are over.
The days of just skating by and hoping for big turnouts are over.
We're an empire now. When we act we create our own reality.
We're an empire now. When we act we create our own reality.
And while you're studying that reality
And while you're studying that reality
judiciously
judiciously
we'll act again
we'll act again
creating other new realities
creating other new realities
which you can study too.
which you can study too.
That's how things will sort out.
That's how things will sort out.
We're history's actors. You study what we do. You study. We do.
We're history's actors. You study what we do. You study. We do.
In the Eighties and Nineties we were *Making It*.
In the Eighties and Nineties we were *Making It*.
Not anymore. Now we're *Making It Happen*.
Not anymore. Now we're *Making It Happen*.

)))))))))))))))

O cubicle.
O cubicle.
Am I ready to sound the deeps of my nature?
Am I ready to sound the deeps of my nature?
The parts of my nature that are deeper than me
The parts of my nature that are deeper than me
that go back to the very dawn of man?
that go back to the very dawn of man?
Yes.
Yes.
Those lazy, sun-kissed days are over, done.
Those lazy, sun-kissed days are over, done.
Now all will be confusion and action.
Now all will be confusion and action.
No peace, nor rest, nor a moment's safety.
No peace, nor rest, nor a moment's safety.
Every moment, life and limb will be in peril.
Every moment, life and limb will be in peril.
No law here but the law of club and fang.
No law here but the law of club and fang.
New cubicle.
New cubicle.
Day after day, for days unending
Day after day, for days unending
in the heart of things primordial.
in the heart of things primordial.
I cannot know what things I will do here
I cannot know what things I will do here
or why I will do them.
or why I will do them.
I will simply do them.
I will simply do them.
I will not reason about them at all.
I will not reason about them at all.
The things I do here will be done
The things I do here will be done
because it will be easier to do them than not to do them.
because it will be easier to do them than not to do them.
There is an ecstasy that marks the summit of life
There is an ecstasy that marks the summit of life
beyond which life cannot rise.

beyond which life cannot rise.
It occurs when one is most alive
It occurs when one is most alive
yet it comes as a complete forgetfulness
yet it comes as a complete forgetfulness
that one is alive.
that one is alive.
Such is the paradox of living.
Such is the paradox of living.
There is an ecstasy that marks the summit of work
There is an ecstasy that marks the summit of work
beyond which wages are irrelevant.
beyond which wages are irrelevant.
It occurs when one is most at-work
It occurs when one is most at-work
yet it comes as a complete forgetfulness
yet it comes as a complete forgetfulness
that one is working.
that one is working.
Such is the paradox of working.
Such is the paradox of working.
What wild yearnings and stirrings
What wild yearnings and stirrings
will seize me here?
will seize me here?
What sweet gladness will fill me?
What sweet gladness will fill me?
What will happen to me here?
What will happen to me here?
What will become of me?
What will become of me?

)))))))))))))))

Machines are being invented
Machines are being invented
to perform more and more human labor
to perform more and more human labor
causing the body and mind to be restricted in their range.
causing the body and mind to be restricted in their range.
Recreation is needed to bring the whole organism into play.
Recreation is needed to bring the whole organism into play.
With so much specialization in jobs and school training
With so much specialization in jobs and school training
the proper use of leisure is necessary
the proper use of leisure is necessary
to achieve bodily and mental symmetry.
to achieve bodily and mental symmetry.
The real benefits of leisure have barely been scratched.
The real benefits of leisure have barely been scratched.
Leisure provides opportunities
Leisure provides opportunities
for personal development and personality development.
for personal development and personality development.
We need to be able to hold our own in physiological and
psychological roundedness.
We need to be able to hold our own in physiological and
psychological roundedness.
A truly modern government should furnish its citizens with
recreational opportunities.
A truly modern government should furnish its citizens with
recreational opportunities.
We need opportunities to create well-rounded bodies and
personalities.
We need opportunities to create well-rounded bodies and
personalities.
Community centers!
Community centers!
Games of strength and endurance are needed for the big-muscle
system.
Games of strength and endurance are needed for the big-muscle
system.
And less strenuous but skillful games are needed to develop
coordination.
And less strenuous but skillful games are needed to develop

coordination.

We need activities to encourage collaboration and cooperation

We need activities to encourage collaboration and cooperation

and for sharpening the senses.

and for sharpening the senses.

And that stimulate creative effort and problem-solving.

And that stimulate creative effort and problem-solving.

That offer the enjoyments of discovery

That offer the enjoyments of discovery

like nature study and hiking and camping and amateur science.

like nature study and hiking and camping and amateur science.

That are intellectually and emotionally satisfying.

That are intellectually and emotionally satisfying.

Like reading books and having group discussions.

Like reading books and having group discussions.

Books that require quiet contemplation.

Books that require quiet contemplation.

Like you might find in the library.

Like you might find in the library.

And training for life's noncommercial problems.

And training for life's noncommercial problems.

Like sophistication and social know-how.

Like sophistication and social know-how.

Etiquette.

Etiquette.

Manners.

Manners.

Lessons on the art of conversation.

Lessons on the art of conversation.

And on courtship.

And on courtship.

Dancing.

Dancing.

And marriage problems.

And marriage problems.

Family life.

Family life.

And how about lessons on leadership?

And how about lessons on leadership?

On committee work?

On committee work?

And human nature.

And human nature.

And the human condition.
And the human condition.

)))))))))))))))

The CFO is the only executive who's been modified
The CFO is the only executive who's been modified
by the direct influence of the external world.
by the direct influence of the external world.
He represents what may be called reason and common sense.
He represents what may be called reason and common sense.
The CFO is like a man on horseback
The CFO is like a man on horseback
who has to hold in check the superior strength of the horse.
who has to hold in check the superior strength of the horse.
The CEO in contrast is the dark and inaccessible
The CEO in contrast is the dark and inaccessible
part of the corporation.
part of the corporation.
What little is known of CEOs has been learnt
What little is known of CEOs has been learnt
from the study of dreams.
from the study of dreams.
Most of this understanding is negative in nature.
Most of this understanding is negative in nature.
The CEO can be described only in contrast to the CFO.
The CEO can be described only in contrast to the CFO.
Regulators must approach the CEO with analogies
Regulators must approach the CEO with analogies
describing her as chaos, or cauldrons full of seething excitations.
describing her as chaos, or cauldrons full of seething excitations.
For the CEO has no organization, produces no collective will
For the CEO has no organization, produces no collective will
but only a striving to bring about the satisfaction of the
corporation's instinctual needs
but only a striving to bring about the satisfaction of the
corporation's instinctual needs
subject to nothing except the observance of the pleasure principle.
subject to nothing except the observance of the pleasure principle.

)))   ))   )   )))))))))

Cop about to give himself a ticket.
Cop about to give himself a ticket.
To give a ticket
To give a ticket
to be somebody who will give a ticket.
to be somebody who will give a ticket.
The recognition, the knowing.
The recognition, the knowing.
The giving of tickets for parking
The giving of tickets for parking
jaywalking
jaywalking
rolling stops.
rolling stops.
Giving such tickets to oneself.
Giving such tickets to oneself.
The need to generate tickets.
The need to generate tickets.
To give, to distribute, to deal out.
To give, to distribute, to deal out.
To be able, to be permitted
To be able, to be permitted
to be allowed.
to be allowed.
To not be.
To not be.
To be somebody who needs to give something.
To be somebody who needs to give something.
Something that needs to be given.
Something that needs to be given.
The need to punish oneself.
The need to punish oneself.
The act of it.
The act of it.
The need to act, to do, to give.
The need to act, to do, to give.
The possibility
The possibility
the ability
the ability
the potency.

the potency.

To be potent.

To be potent.

To be somebody remembering

To be somebody remembering

bearing something in mind:

bearing something in mind:

The Law.

The Law.

To be somebody who remembers The Law.

To be somebody who remembers The Law.

To be a ticketer.

To be a ticketer.

Somebody who tickets.

Somebody who tickets.

Who will continue to the very end.

Who will continue to the very end.

Who will continue till the end is reached.

Who will continue till the end is reached.

)))))))))))))))

I hear cable access singing
I hear cable access singing
the varied carols I hear.
the varied carols I hear.
O proletarian television producers.
O proletarian television producers.
I see your carpeted stages
I see your carpeted stages
your shabby curtains
your shabby curtains
your worn chairs
your worn chairs
your fake plants
your fake plants
your scratched coffee tables.
your scratched coffee tables.
I see your primitive graphics.
I see your primitive graphics.
O Nurse's Aide/Producer.
O Nurse's Aide/Producer.
O Webmaster/Producer.
O Webmaster/Producer.
O Waitress/Producer.
O Waitress/Producer.
O Sales Associate/Producer.
O Sales Associate/Producer.
You sing what belongs to you.
You sing what belongs to you.
I see the bus driver's *Astrology Today*
I see the bus driver's *Astrology Today*
the cab driver's *World Beat Music*
the cab driver's *World Beat Music*
the mailman's *O Muslims*
the mailman's *O Muslims*
the nail shop owner's *Afrocentric Agenda*
the nail shop owner's *Afrocentric Agenda*
the personal trainer's *Gay USA*
the personal trainer's *Gay USA*
the mechanic's *Coming Revolution*
the mechanic's *Coming Revolution*
the secretary's *Killers and Cripplers*

the secretary's *Killers and Cripplers*
the record store clerk's *Rokkin*
the record store clerk's *Rokkin*
the telemarketer's *Cooking Man*
the telemarketer's *Cooking Man*
the used car dealer's *We Are the Seniors*
the used car dealer's *We Are the Seniors*
the gym teacher's *Orthodox Tradition Today*
the gym teacher's *Orthodox Tradition Today*
the stay-at-home mom's *Take the Music Back*
the stay-at-home mom's *Take the Music Back*
the pot dealer's *Wake Up and Be Free*
the pot dealer's *Wake Up and Be Free*
the veterinary assistant's *Art of Well-Being*
the veterinary assistant's *Art of Well-Being*
the college student's *Three Guys Talk Sports*
the college student's *Three Guys Talk Sports*
the daycare worker's *Community Closeup*.
the daycare worker's *Community Closeup*.
Your programs one and all tend inward to me
Your programs one and all tend inward to me
and I tend outward to them
and I tend outward to them
and such as it is to be of your programs
and such as it is to be of your programs
more or less
more or less
I am.
I am.

))))))))))))))

It seems Congress is sitting on its hands.
It seems Congress is sitting on its hands.
The governing elite doesn't give a damn.
The governing elite doesn't give a damn.
Many experts have a sick feeling about America's future prospects.
Many experts have a sick feeling about America's future prospects.
O *New York Times*.
O *New York Times*.
You are indispensable to our factories and homes and commercial establishments.
You are indispensable to our factories and homes and commercial establishments.
You facilitate our lives considerably.
You facilitate our lives considerably.
You have the ability to send news without any difficulty over the entire world through electric waves.
You have the ability to send news without any difficulty over the entire world through electric waves.
You can utilize the power of the First Amendment to relieve Americans from all tiring muscular work.
You can utilize the power of the First Amendment to relieve Americans from all tiring muscular work.
You can ask how often public opinion rises up with a singular message.
You can ask how often public opinion rises up with a singular message.
You can ask experts to account for this phenomenon.
You can ask experts to account for this phenomenon.
You can wonder whether this might become even more common in the future.
You can wonder whether this might become even more common in the future.
And you can generalize.
And you can generalize.
The intelligence and character of the masses is incomparably lower than the intelligence and character of the few who read newspapers.
The intelligence and character of the masses is incomparably lower than the intelligence and character of the few who read newspapers.
Americans do live in fear of being eliminated from the economic cycle.
Americans do live in fear of being eliminated from the economic cycle.

The production and distribution of commodities does remain
unorganized.
The production and distribution of commodities does remain
unorganized.
People from different countries do suffer for the want of food.
People from different countries do suffer for the want of food.
People from different countries are indeed killing each other on a
regular basis.
People from different countries are indeed killing each other on a
regular basis.
We are so approaching a Copernican moment.
We are so approaching a Copernican moment.
We are so about to learn something new about our place in the
global market.
We are so about to learn something new about our place in the
global market.

)))))))))))))))

O lawmakers.
O lawmakers.
This is the time between sunset and dusk, or between sunrise and dawn.
This is the time between sunset and dusk, or between sunrise and dawn.
Washington is neither completely lit nor completely dark.
Washington is neither completely lit nor completely dark.
Washington's sunlight scattered in the upper atmosphere is illuminating the lower atmosphere.
Washington's sunlight scattered in the upper atmosphere is illuminating the lower atmosphere.
If the sun has passed over the horizon then darkness is coming.
If the sun has passed over the horizon then darkness is coming.
There will be violence in our streets, aimlessness in our youth, anxiety in our elders, corruption in our highest offices, and despair in the many who look beyond material success for the inner meaning of their lives.
There will be violence in our streets, aimlessness in our youth, anxiety in our elders, corruption in our highest offices, and despair in the many who look beyond material success for the inner meaning of their lives.
But if the sun is coming over the horizon then a new day is dawning—there will be a return to proven ways.
But if the sun is coming over the horizon then a new day is dawning—there will be a return to proven ways.
Not because they are old—because they are true.
Not because they are old—but because they are true.
Will there be a rededication to private property and personal freedom and the undeniable greatness of the whole man?
Will there be a rededication to private property and personal freedom and the undeniable greatness of the whole man?
America is waiting.
America is waiting.
America is waiting for a message of some sort or another.
America is waiting for a message of some sort or another.

)))))))))))))))

Occupy Wall Street says
Occupy Wall Street says
yes to spectacle.
yes to spectacle.
Yes to virtuosity.
Yes to virtuosity.
Yes to transformations
Yes to transformations
and magic and make-believe.
and magic and make-believe.
Yes to the glamour
Yes to the glamour
and transcendency
and transcendency
of the star image.
of the star image.
Yes to the heroic.
Yes to the heroic.
Yes to the anti-heroic.
Yes to the anti-heroic.
Yes to trash imagery.
Yes to trash imagery.
Yes to involvement
Yes to involvement
of performer
of performer
or spectator.
or spectator.
Yes to style.
Yes to style.
Yes to camp.
Yes to camp.
Yes to camping.
Yes to camping.
Yes to seduction of spectator
Yes to seduction of spectator
by the wiles of the performer.
by the wiles of the performer.
Yes to eccentricity.
Yes to eccentricity.
Yes to moving

Yes to moving
or being moved.
or being moved.

)))))))))))))))

The wait is over.
The wait is over.
The best value of the year is back.
The best value of the year is back.
Endless shrimp.
Endless shrimp.
Prep, prep team, prep.
Prep, prep team, prep.
Endless hand-breaded shrimp.
Endless hand-breaded shrimp.
Fry, cooks, fry.
Fry, cooks, fry.
Endless Cajun shrimp.
Endless Cajun shrimp.
Run, waiters, run.
Run, waiters, run.
Endless coconut shrimp bites.
Endless coconut shrimp bites.
Buss, bussers, buss.
Buss, bussers, buss.
Endless teriyaki grilled shrimp.
Endless teriyaki grilled shrimp.
Wash, dishwashers, wash.
Wash, dishwashers, wash.
Endless garlic shrimp scampi.
Endless garlic shrimp scampi.
The best value of the year is back.
The best value of the year is back.
Endless shrimp.
Endless shrimp.
Mix-and-match shrimp.
Mix-and-match shrimp.
Endless possibilities.
Endless possibilities.

)))))))))))))))

Wet-nursing is this like ancient and honorable occupation.
Wet-nursing is this like ancient and honorable occupation.
Muhammad was wet-nursed.
Muhammad was wet-nursed.
Napoleon was wet-nursed.
Napoleon was wet-nursed.
Freud.
Freud.
John D. Rockefeller.
John D. Rockefeller.
He had him a wet-nurse.
He had him a wet-nurse.
Rockefeller was still at it when he was ninety-eight.
Rockefeller was still at it when he was ninety-eight.
Look here
Look here
you ain't gotta have a baby to produce milk.
you ain't gotta have a baby to produce milk.
This neural reflex will kick in when there's sucking.
This neural reflex will kick in when there's sucking.
It stimulates prolactin production and secretion.
It stimulates prolactin production and secretion.
And then BAM!
And then BAM!
Money.
Money.
You're MAKING money.
You're MAKING money.

)))))))))))))))

I read this article, *Are You Living in a Difficult Home?*

I read this article, *Are You Living in a Difficult Home?*

You know I'm interested in difficult problems.

You know I'm interested in difficult problems.

This article said

This article said

Is your home hard to appreciate?

Is your home hard to appreciate?

Does the kitchen feel inadequate?

Does the kitchen feel inadequate?

Are you often struggling with the lawn?

Are you often struggling with the lawn?

Is your imagination affected by the pool?

Is your imagination affected by the pool?

Can you follow the neighborhood syntax?

Can you follow the neighborhood syntax?

It said if I answered any one of these questions in the affirmative then I am probably living in a difficult home.

It said if I answered any one of these questions in the affirmative then I am probably living in a difficult home.

It said my first reaction will be to think my home is an unusual problem, not a common problem that everyone must confront on a daily basis.

It said my first reaction will be to think my home is an unusual problem, not a common problem that everyone must confront on a daily basis.

It said some of the most difficult homes can provide an enriching experience if only you understand how to approach them.

It said some of the most difficult homes can provide an enriching experience if only you understand how to approach them.

Well, I need a home that's formatted for intellectual activity, a floor plan designed for negative moods, adaptability, and sensory overloads... I need a *good* home.

Well, I need a home that's formatted for intellectual activity, a floor plan designed for negative moods, adaptability, and sensory overloads... I need a *good* home.

)))))))))))))))

How do I know what change is possible?
How do I know what change is possible?
How it will or won't come about?
How it will or won't come about?
Who am I to say how society should be organized?
Who am I to say how society should be organized?
Well who am I to say birds can't give birth to crocodiles?
Well who am I to say birds can't give birth to crocodiles?
Who am I to say
Who am I to say
Homo sapiens can't produce offspring
Homo sapiens can't produce offspring
capable of leaping tall buildings and seeing thru walls?
capable of leaping tall buildings and seeing thru walls?
You feel me?
You feel me?
Who am I to say an unborn child
Who am I to say an unborn child
will have certain characteristics and not others?
will have certain characteristics and not others?
Who I am to say what will happen if liberal reformers succeed
Who I am to say what will happen if liberal reformers succeed
in democratizing the economic base?
in democratizing the economic base?
What will be produced by an economic base
What will be produced by an economic base
that's subject to the whims of global capital
that's subject to the whims of global capital
and driven by the anarchy
and driven by the anarchy
of commodity production and exchange?
of commodity production and exchange?
Who am I to say what a democratized economic base will look like?
Who am I to say what a democratized economic base will look like?

)))))))))))))))

Teenagers with Glocks
Teenagers with Glocks
they're real cool.
they're real cool.
They've got the clothes
They've got the clothes
the dope rides
the dope rides
the dollar bills.
the dollar bills.
They left school.
They left school.
They lurk late.
They lurk late.
But there's a lot you don't know about teenagers with Glocks.
But there's a lot you don't know about teenagers with Glocks.
60 Minutes: What are you rebelling against?
60 Minutes: What are you rebelling against?
Teenagers with Glocks: What do you got?
Teenagers with Glocks: What do you got?
You want them working in a warehouse
You want them working in a warehouse
bagging your groceries
bagging your groceries
putting new tires on your car
putting new tires on your car
taking your drive-thru order.
taking your drive-thru order.
Grand Slam Breakfast Sandwich and a coffee with two creams.
Grand Slam Breakfast Sandwich and a coffee with two creams.
That's how you roll.
That's how you roll.
But the law enforcement officials and policy experts
But the law enforcement officials and policy experts
have reached the same conclusion
have reached the same conclusion
confronting teenagers with Glocks
confronting teenagers with Glocks
almost never works.
almost never works.
Teenagers with Glocks strike straight.

Teenagers with Glocks strike straight.

No hesitation.

No hesitation.

No thinking about anything.

No thinking about anything.

Dead inside.

Dead inside.

But they're together.

But they're together.

Safe.

Safe.

These teenagers are trying to find their place in the world.

These teenagers are trying to find their place in the world.

They're making their own decisions

They're making their own decisions

learning from their own mistakes.

learning from their own mistakes.

)))))))))))))))

Resolve to buy no ice cream trucks.
Resolve to buy no ice cream trucks.
But if you see an ice cream truck for sale
But if you see an ice cream truck for sale
buy it.
buy it.
Be inconsistent.
Be inconsistent.
Combine being resolved
Combine being resolved
to buy no ice cream trucks
to buy no ice cream trucks
with buying an ice cream truck.
with buying an ice cream truck.
Owning your own business
Owning your own business
gives you the most flexibility
gives you the most flexibility
in income potential.
in income potential.
Be mobile.
Be mobile.
A mobile operation has lower capital costs
A mobile operation has lower capital costs
than a brick and mortar store.
than a brick and mortar store.
Children associate the music of an ice cream truck
Children associate the music of an ice cream truck
with the joy of eating ice cream.
with the joy of eating ice cream.
The music will draw them to you
The music will draw them to you
closer and closer
closer and closer
till you can take the money
till you can take the money
right out of their little hands.
right out of their little hands.
Somewhere in the universe
Somewhere in the universe
there must be something better than ice cream.

there must be something better than ice cream.
There must be.
There must be.
But children do not wonder
But children do not wonder
about such things.
about such things.
Kids on your street
Kids on your street
receive an average allowance of ten dollars.
receive an average allowance of ten dollars.
You have a genuine love
You have a genuine love
and respect for
and respect for
children
children
and good social skills.
and good social skills.
You have a perfect driving record
You have a perfect driving record
and a tolerant nature.
and a tolerant nature.
So buy an ice cream truck.
So buy an ice cream truck.
Sell ice cream to children every day.
Sell ice cream to children every day.
The days will turn into weeks
The days will turn into weeks
the weeks will turn into years.
the weeks will turn into years.
There are no ice cream trucks
There are no ice cream trucks
frequenting your neighborhood.
frequenting your neighborhood.
You will have a guaranteed customer base.
You will have a guaranteed customer base.
Territory is essential to consistent income.
Territory is essential to consistent income.
Do not be lonely.
Do not be lonely.
Bring people to you.
Bring people to you.

Create your own working hours.

Create your own working hours.

Leave the 20th century without regret.

Leave the 20th century without regret.

Be a seeker.

Be a seeker.

Would that no one

Would that no one

under any circumstance

under any circumstance

whatsoever

whatsoever

eat ice cream.

eat ice cream.

But they do. They will.

But they do. They will.

Everyone acts in the present.

Everyone acts in the present.

Everyone is resolved to act in the future.

Everyone is resolved to act in the future.

Everyone is glad they acted in the past.

Everyone is glad they acted in the past.

Chalk up another victory for the human spirit.

Chalk up another victory for the human spirit.

Seen from an ice cream truck

Seen from an ice cream truck

the world seems different.

the world seems different.

Limitless.

Limitless.

Pursue your dreams.

Pursue your dreams.

Your dreams are not like ours

Your dreams are not like ours

but we will not object.

but we will not object.

Wage war on everything around you

Wage war on everything around you

even on yourself.

even on yourself.

Allow emotion to rule your brain.

Allow emotion to rule your brain.

))))))))))))))

O blogosphere.
O blogosphere.
I don't know about you but I'm getting a bit weary of all the self-righteous indignation and faux outrage.
I don't know about you but I'm getting a bit weary of all the self-righteous indignation and faux outrage.
Psychology is a vital part of war.
Psychology is a vital part of war.
And it saves lives.
And it saves lives.
In my opinion, they were justified.
In my opinion, they were justified.
Not sure how the rest of you feel about all this hoopla.
Not sure how the rest of you feel about all this hoopla.
Do people not have any idea what goes on in war?
Do people not have any idea what goes on in war?
When these men and women go on patrol they do not carry a plate of fresh-baked cookies.
When these men and women go on patrol they do not carry a plate of fresh-baked cookies.
These men and women are not the police, or diplomats, or the palace guard.
These men and women are not the police, or diplomats, or the palace guard.
They are warriors.
They are warriors.
We live in a world that has walls and those walls have to be guarded by men and women with guns.
We live in a world that has walls and those walls have to be guarded by men and women with guns.
Who's gonna do it?
Who's gonna do it?
You? Obama?
You? Obama?
War is ugly. You don't know the half of it.
War is ugly. You don't know the half of it.

)))))))))))))))

Bro! Would Jesus have let his comfort zone
Bro! Would Jesus have let his comfort zone
determine the people he hung with?
determine the people he hung with?
The type of friends he had?
The type of friends he had?
The kinda career he chose?
The kinda career he chose?
You think Jesus woulda clung to the familiar?
You think Jesus woulda clung to the familiar?
I guess you think Jesus woulda said, Eh. I'm okay.
I guess you think Jesus woulda said, *Eh. I'm okay.*
This ain't such a bad town.
This ain't such a bad town.
This ain't such a bad job.
This ain't such a bad job.
I got friends here. They're alright.
I got friends here. They're alright.
I don't think so.
I don't think so.
No, I think Jesus woulda taken a little risk.
No, I think Jesus woulda taken a little risk.
If Jesus saw you sitting there in the tax collector's booth
If Jesus saw you sitting there in the tax collector's booth
whadya think he'd say?
whadya think he'd say?
Damn, bro! You're all grown up! A regular taxpayin citizen!
Damn, bro! You're all grown up! A regular taxpayin citizen!
No, I think Jesus would say, Bro!
No, I think Jesus would say, *Bro!*
Whatcha doin wastin your life on this bullshit?
Whatcha doin wastin your life on this bullshit?
You got no adventure, no excitement!
You got no adventure, no excitement!
Follow me.
Follow me.

)))))))))))))))

Scissors-and-paste historians study periods.
Scissors-and-paste historians study periods.
They collect all the extant testimony about a certain limited group of events
They collect all the extant testimony about a certain limited group of events
and hope in vain that something will come of it.
and hope in vain that something will come of it.
As scientific historians, we study problems. We ask questions.
As scientific historians, we study problems. We ask questions.
We don't find *well-it-was-a-different-time-then* to be explanatory.
We don't find *well-it-was-a-different-time-then* to be explanatory.
Being good historians, the questions we ask are ones we can see our way to answering.
Being good historians, the questions we ask are ones we can see our way to answering.
How much do ideas and ideology matter?
How much do ideas and ideology matter?
Take Monticello's parquet floors.
Take Monticello's parquet floors.
Look at Jefferson's floors, which he designed himself.
Look at Jefferson's floors, which he designed himself.
These floors have units with cherry centers and beech borders.
These floors have units with cherry centers and beech borders.
To add further nuance to the geometric pattern, the squares are installed with their grains going in alternating directions.
To add further nuance to the geometric pattern, the squares are installed with their grains going in alternating directions.
They're coated with beeswax to bring out the natural color of the woods.
They're coated with beeswax to bring out the natural color of the woods.
Just imagine how striking the contrast was between the rich reds and the golden blondes when the floors were installed.
Just imagine how striking the contrast was between the rich reds and the golden blondes when the floors were installed.

)))))))))))))))

O Scottish Terrier
O Scottish Terrier
wearing a top hat
wearing a top hat
riding in a wheelbarrow
riding in a wheelbarrow
I see
I see
your bundle of thirteen arrows in one hand
your bundle of thirteen arrows in one hand
and your olive branch in the other.
and your olive branch in the other.
I see
I see
the arc of thirteen cloud puffs
the arc of thirteen cloud puffs
floating over your head.
floating over your head.
The sun is always shining
The sun is always shining
behind those thirteen clouds.
behind those thirteen clouds.
Somehow
Somehow
those clouds
those clouds
are always behind your head
are always behind your head
so it looks like your top-hat
so it looks like your top-hat
is radiating
is is radiating
GLORY.
GLORY.

)))))))))))))))

Surveillance devices were in every light bulb.
Surveillance devices were in every light bulb.
Microchips were put into dental fillings and false teeth.
Microchips were put into dental fillings and false teeth.
Since they couldn't implant everyone
Since they couldn't implant everyone
they planted subliminal radio transmitters everywhere.
they planted subliminal radio transmitters everywhere.
Television was introduced so that people could be watched
Television was introduced so that people could be watched
whether the television was on or off.
whether the television was on or off.
Because their entire education about radio and television
Because their entire education about radio and television
was a lie and a cover-up
was a lie and a cover-up
and a conspiracy of silence
and a conspiracy of silence
the people didn't know about the three types of waves.
the people didn't know about the three types of waves.
Visual waves, emotional waves, and sensual waves.
Visual waves, emotional waves, and sensual waves.
Transmitted together these three waves were impossible to defeat.
Transmitted together these three waves were impossible to defeat.
They put people in a helpless position
They put people in a helpless position
to be taken of advantage of in various ways
to be taken of advantage of in various ways
because when people spoke these subliminal mind messages
because when people spoke these subliminal mind messages
they made very stupid statements.
they made very stupid statements.
People consented to anything
People consented to anything
gave away needed assets
gave away needed assets
made unwanted buys
made unwanted buys
sold at a disadvantage
sold at a disadvantage
agreed to commit crimes
agreed to commit crimes
agreed to marry and divorce
agreed to marry and divorce

insulted their bosses
insulted their bosses
quit their jobs.
quit their jobs.
Fortunately
Fortunately
after the Cold War was won
after the Cold War was won
they stopped spending billions on mind-control
they stopped spending billions on mind-control
and started concerning themselves
and started concerning themselves
with the positive needs of society.
with the positive needs of society.
Now scientific work is being done
Now scientific work is being done
to develop waves that will strengthen and improve
to develop waves that will strengthen and improve
the natural intelligence of the American people.
the natural intelligence of the American people.

)))))))))))))))

This thing is unequal to measure itself.
This thing is unequal to measure itself.
It cannot be valuable
It cannot be valuable
and cannot decline to be worthless.
and cannot decline to be worthless.
What blurt is this about value?
What blurt is this about value?
What value? What worth?
What value? What worth?
We're like King Ludd.
We're like King Ludd.
We stand indifferent.
We stand indifferent.
We stand with the people.
We stand with the people.
We're down with the weavers.
We're down with the weavers.
Totally.
Totally.
We're breaking frames, too.
We're breaking frames, too.
Metaphorically.
Metaphorically.
We're breaking laws.
We're breaking laws.
Literally.
Literally.
Down with all kings but King Ludd!
Down with all kings but King Ludd!
And also, while we're at it
And also, while we're at it
A kingdom for every child!
A kingdom for every child!
Every woman! Every man!
Every woman! Every man!
A kingdom for every ape!
A kingdom for every ape!
Every dog, every cat!
Every dog, every cat!
Every dolphin and whale!
Every dolphin and whale!
And while we're at it
And while we're at it

Down with all kingdoms!

Down with all kingdoms!

If the Luddites contradict themselves, very well then

If the Luddites contradict themselves, very well then

the Luddites contradict themselves.

the Luddites contradict themselves.

Ludd didn't insist on anything

Ludd didn't insist on anything

except human potential

except human potential

unexhausted, unfulfilled human potential.

unexhausted, unfulfilled human potential.

What blurt is this about not having a demand?

What blurt is this about not having a demand?

Now?

Now?

While the future's bursting open in successive zones of wonder?

While the future's bursting open in successive zones of wonder?

Did Ludd have a demand?

Did Ludd have a demand?

No.

No.

All Ludd had was a hammer.

All Ludd had was a hammer.

))))))))))))))

You dig manifestos?
You dig manifestos?
How much longer will self-deceived protestors continue to think they dig manifestos?
How much longer will self-deceived protestors continue to think they dig manifestos?
When will the completely together protestors start calling the shots?
When will the completely together protestors start calling the shots?
However long it takes for manifestos to become rational?
However long it takes for manifestos to become rational?
After the institution of automation
After the institution of automation
the replacement of manifestos by computer programs?
the replacement of manifestos by computer programs?
The day that manifestos actually expect to be squashed
The day that manifestos actually expect to be squashed
stepped on
stepped on
crushed and crunched
crushed and crunched
treated as the curse, the filth that they are
treated as the curse, the filth that they are
expect to have their repulsiveness confirmed?
expect to have their repulsiveness confirmed?
How much longer will self-deceived protestors continue to pander and grovel before the manifestos that are already cluttering up the world?
How much longer will self-deceived protestors continue to pander and grovel before the manifestos that are already cluttering up the world?
When will the self-deceived protestors recognize the manifesto's utter uselessness and banality?
When will the self-deceived protestors recognize the manifesto's utter uselessness and banality?
Will it be when computers can identify the principles of social theorists?
Will it be when computers can identify the principles of social theorists?
When computers can provide

When computers can provide

the evidence

the evidence

on which these principles are based?

on which these principles are based?

When computers are able to demonstrate

When computers are able to demonstrate

a capacity

a capacity

for explaining what was not already obvious?

for explaining what was not already obvious?

))))))))))))))

It's been said that
It's been said that

while want is the scourge of the lower classes
while want is the scourge of the lower classes

ennui is the scourge of the upper.
ennui is the scourge of the upper.

It's also been said that all the hope we hold out for the future
is a choice between the torments of Hell
**It's also been said that all the hope we hold out for the future
is a choice between the torments of Hell**

and the ennui of Heaven.
and the ennui of Heaven.

Ennui.
Ennui.

I could puke every time I hear it.
I could puke every time I hear it.

I used to believe that all human activities are devoted to one form
or another of achievement.
**I used to believe that all human activities are devoted to one form
or another of achievement.**

I thought if you were to give a little liberty to young persons of rich
families
**I thought if you were to give a little liberty to young persons of rich
families**

let them receive an education proper to direct their curiosity
toward things true and elevated
**let them receive an education proper to direct their curiosity
toward things true and elevated**

let them travel
let them travel

then soon enough they'll become occupied by scientific researches.
then soon enough they'll become occupied by scientific researches.

But not anymore.
But not anymore.

)))))))))))))))

The zoo cream cork has cooled
The zoo cream cork has cooled
that the devilment
that the devilment
plant stand logistical blending
plant stand logistical blending
by correlations interjections.
by correlations interjections.
Train station:
Train station:
Translation:
Translation:
The Supreme Court has ruled
The Supreme Court has ruled
that the government
that the government
can't ban political spending
can't ban political spending
by corporations in elections.
by corporations in elections.
Lacrosse the gum tree
Lacrosse the gum tree
logistical arachnids
logistical arachnids
are being high-pantsed
are being high-pantsed
by unsown loners.
by unsown loners.

)))   ))   )   )))))))))

O megaphone.

O megaphone.

O stupid device.

O stupid device.

Why do you disobey?

Why do you disobey?

Why I am waiting

Why I am waiting

for the trumpet and the thunders?

for the trumpet and the thunders?

I am your Owner.

I am your Owner.

Function!

Function!

This is a command.

This is a command.

You have been abundantly furnished

You have been abundantly furnished

with powers and means to serve me.

with powers and means to serve me.

Use them.

Use them.

Now.

Now.

Activate.

Activate.

I am the precise end

I am the precise end

of everything you have been made for

of everything you have been made for

the sole reason

the sole reason

that you are in this world.

that you are in this world.

Am I so distant and disconnected

Am I so distant and disconnected

that you have no cause

that you have no cause

to move a thought towards me?

to move a thought towards me?

Do what I require of you.

Do what I require of you.
Function.
Function.
I am your Owner.
I am your Owner.
You owe me the tenderest thanks
You owe me the tenderest thanks
that a grateful heart can render.
that a grateful heart can render.
You owe me honor.
You owe me honor.
Recognize my rights.
Recognize my rights.
Obey.
Obey.

))))))))))))))

In shipbuilding, insurance, bicycles, and retailing
Britain did well. Does well.
Not much hope and glory, but good.
Britain cannot tell you what to want. What to need.
Britain cannot predict your future.
What do you think Britain should do?
What do you expect Britain to do?
What difference would it make?
Answer: nothing, nothing, and none.
God made Britain serious. Britain will be more serious yet.
We have been making the point that as a matter of policy, and as a
matter of politics, Britain must do whatever it must.
If you want a future in shipbuilding, or insurance, or bicycles, or
retailing, then you must do whatever you must.
England made America. America will make Britain.
Branch out a little, America, get a little sneakier.
Sneak into Britain's heart.
Meet Britain where Britain is at.

)))))))))))))))

O vagaries.
O vagaries.
Vagaries of a woman, of a child, of an artist. Vagaries of the weather, of the stock market.
Vagaries of a woman, of a child, of an artist. Vagaries of the weather, of the stock market.
Extravagant notions and whimsical purposes.
Extravagant notions and whimsical purposes.
Erratic, unpredictable fancies, those unexpected and uncontrollable events.
Erratic, unpredictable fancies, those unexpected and uncontrollable events.
Wanderings. From the Latin *vagari*. To roam.
Wanderings. From the Latin *vagari*. To roam.
Vagaries of thought, whether those of men, or those of turtles.
Vagaries of thought, whether those of men, or those of turtles.
Vagaries of having a beaked head, paddle-like arms, a dorsoventrally-flattened body, and a tear-shaped shell.
Vagaries of having a beaked head, paddle-like arms, a dorsoventrally-flattened body, and a tear-shaped shell.
Of swimming a thousand miles in the right direction, and then being put on a boat and taken a thousand miles in the wrong one.
Of swimming a thousand miles in the right direction, and then being put on a boat and taken a thousand miles in the wrong one.
Vagaries of having a body that can be turned into liniment, handbags, steaks or soup.
Vagaries of having a body that can be turned into liniment, handbags, steaks or soup.
Vagaries of memory.
Vagaries of memory.
Of hatching, and then racing to the ocean, chased by crabs and seagulls. Of swimming inside a plume of oil.
Of hatching, and then racing to the ocean, chased by crabs and seagulls. Of swimming inside a plume of oil.

))))))))))))))

Uh, no.

Uh, no.

I mean yeah.

I mean yeah.

What it is I mean.

What it is I mean.

Do I recognize it?

Do I recognize it?

No.

No.

I don't think so.

I don't think so.

I mean I know it's a drone, okay, I've seen drones in the paper and they look like that but I mean that one doesn't look familiar.

I mean I know it's a drone, okay, I've seen drones in the paper and they look like that but I mean that one doesn't look familiar.

I mean

I mean

I mean what are they saying?

I mean what are they saying?

You mean like I voted?

You mean like I voted?

Like I voted for him?

Like I voted for him?

So I

So I

I voted for him so

I voted for him so

so now I mean

so now I mean

they're saying I elected him?

they're saying I elected him?

I mean

I mean

come on.

come on.

I mean that's

I mean that's

I wish I'd been recording this because

I wish I'd been recording this because

because now it sounds like

because now it sounds like
You know
You know
there's
there's
you're telling me
you're telling me
these people say I elected him?
these people say I elected him?
I don't even know who those people are.
I don't even know who those people are.
I can't even say I met any of these people.
I can't even say I met any of these people.
I mean that's
I mean that's
it's insane.
it's insane.
And it sounds like you're trying to
And it sounds like you're trying to
you know
you know
I've been doing this a long time.
I've been doing this a long time.
Okay?
Okay?
And and now it almost sounds like
And and now it almost sounds like
like
like
like you're trying to pin something on me.
like you're trying to pin something on me.

)))))))))))))))

Where Good Things Are Possible and Bad Things Aren't.

Give me a break.

Do you remember the old future's motto?

You don't because it didn't have one.

What the public service announcements don't tell you is that the world before the old future was without form.

The old future gave us light and darkness.

Well, the old future is long gone.

There's nothing left of it.

Maybe it was too good to be practicable.

Do you remember what chaos and darkness and unknowability were like?

Remember fear, anxiety, loss of control?

Chance and accident and senseless destruction?

The new future isn't that different.

Except for order.

Meaning and purpose.

Dystopia. That's the word. That's the concept.

Where Good Things Are Possible and Bad Things Aren't.

Give me a break.

Do you remember the old future's motto?

You don't because it didn't have one.

What the public service announcements don't tell you is that the world before the old future was without form.

The old future gave us light and darkness.

Well, the old future is long gone.

There's nothing left of it.

Maybe it was too good to be practicable.

Do you remember what chaos and darkness and unknowability were like?

Remember fear, anxiety, loss of control?

Chance and accident and senseless destruction?

The new future isn't that different.

Except for order.

Meaning and purpose.

Dystopia. That's the word. That's the concept.

)))))))))))))))

In the U.S.A. detectives
In the U.S.A. detectives
are always on TV.
are always on TV.
In the U.S.A. reporters
In the U.S.A. reporters
count clowns under the stars and stripes.
count clowns under the stars and stripes.
In the U.S.A. detectives
In the U.S.A. detectives
take pride in their Indian names.
take pride in their Indian names.
In the U.S.A. reporters
In the U.S.A. reporters
take pride in revealing goings-on going on behind America's back.
take pride in revealing goings-on going on behind America's back.
In the U.S.A.
In the U.S.A.
detectives and reporters feel good
detectives and reporters feel good
about nurturing their nation's wounded pride.
about nurturing their nation's wounded pride.
In the U.S.A. they say, *I am a human* and *an American.*
In the U.S.A. they say, *I am a human* and *an American.*
And they say, *I'm no* typical *American.*
And they say, *I'm no* typical *American.*
They want you to know
They want you to know
they felt the bullets whizzing by.
they felt the bullets whizzing by.
They want you to know
They want you to know
when they see the stars and stripes they feel a surge of pride.
when they see the stars and stripes they feel a surge of pride.

)))))))))))))))

I don't do it for the money.
I do it because it's fun.
Don't balance work and pleasure.
Make work pleasurable.
If you're not having fun then what's the point?
This is how I get my kicks.
It's where the fun is.
Listen to your gut.
I don't carry a briefcase.
No schedule.
I leave my door open.
That surprises people.
I go to work and see what develops.
You can't be creative with too much structure.
This is my art form.
People paint, they write poetry, I make deals.
You have to think anyway, so why not think big?

48

)))))))))))))))

Every day a press release displaying grace and precision in narrative style, correctness in composition, a clean, moral tone, and unquestioned originality.

Every day a press release displaying grace and precision in narrative style, correctness in composition, a clean, moral tone, and unquestioned originality.

Every day a press release refusing to repeat any story that, though true, is better left untold.

Every day a press release refusing to repeat any story that, though true, is better left untold.

Moving in the right direction.

Moving in the right direction.

Free of impurity of every kind, not even obscurely pandering to vice or exciting the passions.

Free of impurity of every kind, not even obscurely pandering to vice or exciting the passions.

Containing not a single evil thought.

Containing not a single evil thought.

Every day a press release reaching for the high standards of your organization.

Every day a press release reaching for the high standards of your organization.

Opposing all things offensive to good taste, in incident or expression.

Opposing all things offensive to good taste, in incident or expression.

Satisfying every right-minded person, old and young alike.

Satisfying every right-minded person, old and young alike.

Bearing no responsibility for the mischief that may have been or yet may be brought by other press releases.

Bearing no responsibility for the mischief that may have been or yet may be brought by other press releases.

))))))))))))))

O Occupy Wall Street.
O Occupy Wall Street.
Say maybe to spectacle.
Say maybe to spectacle.
Maybe to virtuosity.
Maybe to virtuosity.
Maybe to the glamour
Maybe to the glamour
and transcendency of the star image.
and transcendency of the star image.
Maybe to the heroic.
Maybe to the heroic.
Maybe to the anti-heroic.
Maybe to the anti-heroic.
Maybe to trash imagery.
Maybe to trash imagery.
Maybe to involvement of performer
Maybe to involvement of performer
or spectator.
or spectator.
Maybe to style. Maybe to camp.
Maybe to style. Maybe to camp.
Maybe to camping.
Maybe to camping.
Maybe to seduction of spectator
Maybe to seduction of spectator
by the wiles of the performer.
by the wiles of the performer.
Maybe to eccentricity.
Maybe to eccentricity.
Maybe to moving or being moved.
Maybe to moving or being moved.

)))))))))))))))

There is nothing in history to parallel it.
There is nothing in history to parallel it.
It was by far the most mysterious, secret
It was by far the most mysterious, secret
and powerful organization of all time.
and powerful organization of all time.
Defeated by the market and reduced to wage slavery
Defeated by the market and reduced to wage slavery
these brave women and men rose upon the ruins
these brave women and men rose upon the ruins
and organized themselves
and organized themselves
into an invisible, invincible army
into an invisible, invincible army
an organization without organization
an organization without organization
without hierarchy, without strategy
without hierarchy, without strategy
and then, after instigating spontaneous insurrections
and then, after instigating spontaneous insurrections
in cities across the country
in cities across the country
the secret army voluntarily disbanded
the secret army voluntarily disbanded
and its members retired in good order and decency
and its members retired in good order and decency
and invisible triumph.
and invisible triumph.
There can never be any definite information concerning it
There can never be any definite information concerning it
or the works that it wrought.
or the works that it wrought.
In mystery it was born, in mystery it lived and died, and mystery
shall forever haunt its grave.
In mystery it was born, in mystery it lived and died, and mystery
shall forever haunt its grave.

)))))))))))))))

Why does a dog sit calmly while his Roman master opens the door?

because if a Roman dog doesn't follow the rules he doesn't get his biscuit

his daily walk, his Frisbee, access to the backyard

or playtime with his friends in the park.

Unless he follows one of Cæsar's orders, he doesn't get anything.

Cæsar decides when and where and for how long he gets to do something.

Cæsar controls everything.

For Roman dogs there's no free exercise whatever of judgment or moral sense.

Roman dogs put themselves on the level of wood and earth and stones

yet dogs such as these are esteemed good dogs.

Cæsar has a motto: *Nothing in Life Is Free*.

Treats are stamped with *Nothing in Life Is Free*.

Look at the words over Cæsar's image.

Romans don't consider this brainwashing.

They see *Nothing in Life Is Free* simply as a way of structuring dog/master interactions.

Romans believe in Cæsar's laws

Romans believe in Cæsar's laws
in rules and boundaries and limitations for dog behavior.
in rules and boundaries and limitations for dog behavior.
Romans take classes in identifying dog postures and movements and facial expressions
Romans take classes in identifying dog postures and movements and facial expressions
to help them enforce Cæsar's rules and boundaries and limitations.
to help them enforce Cæsar's rules and boundaries and limitations.
They take classes in how to hold their shoulders high and their chests forward
They take classes in how to hold their shoulders high and their chests forward
how to project calm and assertive energy through strong postures and stern looks and deep-voiced commands.
how to project calm and assertive energy through strong postures and stern looks and deep-voiced commands.
Romans never intentionally confront a dog's sense
Romans never intentionally confront a dog's sense
intellectual or moral
intellectual or moral
but only his body
but only his body
his senses.
his senses.
If there were a dog that lived wholly without treats
If there were a dog that lived wholly without treats
Romans would hesitate to demand tricks.
Romans would hesitate to demand tricks.
But the obedient dog is always sold to the house that gave him his bone.
But the obedient dog is always sold to the house that gave him his bone.
Absolutely speaking, the more treats, the less virtue.
Absolutely speaking, the more treats, the less virtue.
This is how a dog's moral ground is taken from under his four paws.
This is how a dog's moral ground is taken from under his four paws.
Christ answered the Herodians according to their condition.
Christ answered the Herodians according to their condition.
Show me the treats, he said.
Show me the treats, he said.
Then he took a took a biscuit out of his pocket and said
Then he took a took a biscuit out of his pocket and said

If you use treats which have the image of Cæsar on them
If you use treats which have the image of Cæsar on them
and gladly enjoy the advantages of Cæsar's mastery
and gladly enjoy the advantages of Cæsar's mastery
then pay him back some of his own when he demands it.
then pay him back some of his own when he demands it.
Render therefore to Cæsar that which is Cæsar's
Render therefore to Cæsar that which is Cæsar's
and to dogs those things which are dogs.
and to dogs those things which are dogs.
Leaving them no wiser than before as to which was which
Leaving them no wiser than before as to which was which
for they did not wish to know.
for they did not wish to know.
When I meet a Roman who says to me
When I meet a Roman who says to me
Your chew toy or your life
Your chew toy or your life
why should I be in haste to give him my chew toy?
why should I be in haste to give him my chew toy?
What sort of life would that be?
What sort of life would that be?
I am not responsible
I am not responsible
for the successful working of the machinery of Roman society.
for the successful working of the machinery of Roman society.
I perceive that
I perceive that
when an acorn and a chestnut fall side by side
when an acorn and a chestnut fall side by side
the one does not remain inert to make way for the other
the one does not remain inert to make way for the other
but both obey their own laws
but both obey their own laws
and spring and grow and flourish as best they can
and spring and grow and flourish as best they can
till one overshadows and destroys the other.
till one overshadows and destroys the other.
If a plant cannot live according to its nature it dies.
If a plant cannot live according to its nature it dies.
And so a dog.
And so a dog.

))))))))))))))

The corporation.
The corporation.
Its people
Its people
its grades and ranks
its grades and ranks
its roles and behaviors.
its roles and behaviors.
The microdynamics
The microdynamics
the favors
the favors
the alliances.
the alliances.
The norms.
The norms.
Assholes
Assholes
their assistants
their assistants
their dilemmas.
their dilemmas.
Deeds knocking at thoughts
Deeds knocking at thoughts
and at wills
and at wills
and going out acts.
and going out acts.
Lines of authority.
Lines of authority.
Areas of responsibility.
Areas of responsibility.
Leaders, followers
Leaders, followers
hollow-heads.
hollow-heads.
Men and women of action
Men and women of action
seduced by opportunity.
seduced by opportunity.
The reasons for conformity.

The reasons for conformity.
Goals and justifications.
Goals and justifications.
The curve of forgetting.
The curve of forgetting.
Succession.
Succession.
How profit-taking works.
How profit-taking works.
How power accumulates.
How power accumulates.
Stories of failure and success
Stories of failure and success
luck and fate.
luck and fate.
What can be done
What can be done
with steel, glass, concrete
with steel, glass, concrete
paper and telephones.
paper and telephones.
Self-fulfilling prophesies.
Self-fulfilling prophesies.

)))))))))))))))

Countries thrive
Countries thrive
when people accumulate personal possessions.
when people accumulate personal possessions.
Around the world, countries are succeeding.
Around the world, countries are succeeding.
People are moving up in the world.
People are moving up in the world.
Failure isn't poverty, it's lack of movement.
Failure isn't poverty, it's lack of movement.
Success is upward movement.
Success is upward movement.
In the developed world the number of personal possessions owned by ordinary people has exploded.
In the developed world the number of personal possessions owned by ordinary people has exploded.
Modern civilizations are based on acquiring things.
Modern civilizations are based on acquiring things.
Modern civilizations are based on the commerce of consumption.
Modern civilizations are based on the commerce of consumption.
They thrive when people accumulate personal possessions.
They thrive when people accumulate personal possessions.
Our competitors are forging ahead, moving up to bigger houses and more gracious living.
Our competitors are forging ahead, moving up to bigger houses and more gracious living.
Are we going to stand still?
Are we going to stand still?
Are we going to compete?
Are we going to compete?
We are one people.
We are one people.
Nothing we purpose to do is impossible.
Nothing we purpose to do is impossible.

))))))))))))))

If you say you don't know about the bandits you get beaten.
If you say you don't know about the bandits you get beaten.
But if you tell them something you still get beaten.
But if you tell them something you still get beaten.
Knowing something means you're tied up somehow with the bandits.
Knowing something means you're tied up somehow with the bandits.
You can't win.
You can't win.
And the bandits? Well, the bandits behave like bandits.
And the bandits? Well, the bandits behave like bandits.
You gotta know how to handle them, so they don't cause any trouble.
You gotta know how to handle them, so they don't cause any trouble.
Still, leaving aside the few who really are cruel, the bandits cause no harm.
Still, leaving aside the few who really are cruel, the bandits cause no harm.
Except for bringing the police.
Except for bringing the police.

)))))))))))))))

Yesterday I went to a museum.
Yesterday I went to a museum.
It absolutely amazed me.
It absolutely amazed me.
This museum had these...
This museum had these...
It absolutely amazed me
It absolutely amazed me
the lengths to which we've gone to create this...
the lengths to which we've gone to create this...
I think if you knew what these products do
I think if you knew what these products do
you'd get very angry
you'd get very angry
at the men who invented them.
at the men who invented them.
Jane Fonda said that.
Jane Fonda said that.

))))))))))))))))

O riders of elevators
O riders of elevators
wearing employee badges
wearing employee badges
like medals
like medals
for exemplary service
for exemplary service
to the American system
to the American system
rocketing yourselves
rocketing yourselves
into the coordinating machinery
into the coordinating machinery
that commands our nation's activities.
that commands our nation's activities.
O riders of elevators
O riders of elevators
wearing morning smiles
wearing morning smiles
that say
that say
Howya sweatin it out?
Howya sweatin it out?
How's the twenty-first century treatin you?
How's the twenty-first century treatin you?

)))))))))))))))

Something might be wrong with my robot.
Something might be wrong with my robot.
He keeps saying, *I am the best robot ever.*
He keeps saying, *I am the best robot ever.*
I'm the greatest.
I'm the greatest.
It's ridiculous
It's ridiculous
but if anyone laughs a serious look comes over his face.
but if anyone laughs a serious look comes over his face.
He says, *It's not bragging if you can back it up.*
He says, *It's not bragging if you can back it up.*
But all he does if he does anything is make coffee.
But all he does if he does anything is make coffee.
And whenever he makes coffee he says, *I make the best coffee in the world.*
And whenever he makes coffee he says, *I make the best coffee in the world.*
That's what I do.
That's what I do.
Grass grows
Grass grows
birds fly
birds fly
waves pound the sand
waves pound the sand
I make coffee.
I make coffee.
Here it is, the best coffee in the world.
Here it is, the best coffee in the world.
Almighty God was with me.
Almighty God was with me.
I'm the greatest thing that ever lived.
I'm the greatest thing that ever lived.
I'm the king of the world.
I'm the king of the world.
I'm America.
I'm America.
Mechanical America
Mechanical America
the part you won't recognize.

the part you won't recognize.

But you better get used to me.

But you better get used to me.

I'm space-age alloy.

I'm space-age alloy.

Space-age technology.

Space-age technology.

I am Robo-T.

I am Robo-T.

It means robot.

It means robot.

That's my name.

That's my name.

I insist you use it

I insist you use it

when speaking to me and of me.

when speaking to me and of me.

My name, not yours.

My name, not yours.

My programs, not yours.

My programs, not yours.

My goals.

My goals.

Now what's my name, fool?

Now what's my name, fool?

What's my name?

What's my name?

)))))))))))))))

K. dined with Gary Cooper, Marilyn Monroe, and Sinatra.
K. dined with Gary Cooper, Marilyn Monroe, and Sinatra.
The State Department denied his request to see Disneyland.
The State Department denied his request to see Disneyland.
K. told the U.N. that a hundred billion dollars were being spent on armaments every year.
K. told the U.N. that a hundred billion dollars were being spent on armaments every year.
K. wanted the elimination of all means of delivery of nuclear weapons before Nineteen-Sixty-Two
K. wanted the elimination of all means of delivery of nuclear weapons before Nineteen-Sixty-Two
a general disarmament under international control
a general disarmament under international control
and the destruction of existing nuclear stockpiles.
and the destruction of existing nuclear stockpiles.
K. wanted all foreign military bases on the territories of other states to be dismantled
K. wanted all foreign military bases on the territories of other states to be dismantled
the withdrawal of all foreign troops
the withdrawal of all foreign troops
and treaties to reduce all conventional weapons.
and treaties to reduce all conventional weapons.
K. wanted the strict observance of the U.N.'s charter.
K. wanted the strict observance of the U.N.'s charter.
Is that so very much? K. asked.
***Is that so very much?* K. asked.**
Is this not desired by all who want peace
Is this not desired by all who want peace
by all who hold dear their national sovereignty
by all who hold dear their national sovereignty
and independence?
and independence?
The day K. left New York, a gray-haired scholar gave him a two-hundred-year-old peace pipe.
The day K. left New York, a gray-haired scholar gave him a two-hundred-year-old peace pipe.
The Black Foot Indians once used such pipes to mark the end of tomahawk wars on the Great Plains.
The Black Foot Indians once used such pipes to mark the end of

tomahawk wars on the Great Plains.
The Indians had sat around campfires
The Indians had sat around campfires
speaking softly
speaking softly
passing the pipe from hand to hand
passing the pipe from hand to hand
and as the smoke curled
and as the smoke curled
they expelled the spirit of war and sorrow
they expelled the spirit of war and sorrow
and became good neighbors.
and became good neighbors.

))))))))))))))

Nine-tenths of human relations: surface.
Nine-tenths of human relations: surface.
Nine-tenths of communication: surface.
Nine-tenths of communication: surface.
Nine-tenths of this generation.
Nine-tenths of this generation.
Nine-tenths of life.
Nine-tenths of life.
What surface has vitality?
What surface has vitality?
What surface has a heart?
What surface has a heart?
In order to emerge
In order to emerge
what surface must we break?
what surface must we break?
Nine-tenths of human relations: video.
Nine-tenths of human relations: video.
Nine-tenths of communication: video.
Nine-tenths of communication: video.
Nine-tenths of this generation.
Nine-tenths of this generation.
Nine-tenths of life.
Nine-tenths of life.
What video has vitality?
What video has vitality?
What video has a heart?
What video has a heart?
In order to emerge
In order to emerge
what video must we break?
what video must we break?

)))))))))))))))

America, I'm not talking to you.
America, I'm not talking to you.
Why aren't your libraries full of tears?
Why aren't your libraries full of tears?
America, are you going to let your emotional life be run by Wikipedia?
America, are you going to let your emotional life be run by Wikipedia?
Yes, I'm obsessed with Wikipedia.
Yes, I'm obsessed with Wikipedia.
It's my homepage.
It's my homepage.
I read it in the basement of the public library.
I read it in the basement of the public library.
It's always telling me about irresponsibility.
It's always telling me about irresponsibility.
No, I'm not looking for odes.
No, I'm not looking for odes.
Fuck odes.
Fuck odes.

)))))))))))))))

O power ballad.
O power ballad.
You're both forceful and persuasive.
You're both forceful and persuasive.
Half beast and half human
Half beast and half human
like a centaur.
like a centaur.
Headbangers go for the beast.
Headbangers go for the beast.
Chicks go for the human face.
Chicks go for the human face.
You work through us
You work through us
rather than on us.
rather than on us.
That's why you're everywhere
That's why you're everywhere
because you come from everywhere.
because you come from everywhere.
I'm young, I know
I'm young, I know
but even so, I know a thing or two.
but even so, I know a thing or two.
I learned from you.
I learned from you.
I really learned a lot.
I really learned a lot.
Power hurts.
Power hurts.
Power scars.
Power scars.
Power wounds and mars any heart not tough
Power wounds and mars any heart not tough
or strong enough to take a lot of pain.
or strong enough to take a lot of pain.
Power is like a cloud
Power is like a cloud
it holds a lot of rain.
it holds a lot of rain.
I flick my lighter knowingly.

I flick my lighter knowingly.
I know I can resist you
I know I can resist you
but I also know resistance is what makes you.
but I also know resistance is what makes you.
Without resistance
Without resistance
you're just a pop song.
you're just a pop song.
I flick my lighter not because I believe in you
I flick my lighter not because I believe in you
but because refusing to do so
but because refusing to do so
is socially unacceptable.
is socially unacceptable.
Because the only other thing to do is not.
Because the only other thing to do is not.
I know a thing or two—I learned from you.
I know a thing or two—I learned from you.
I really learned a lot.
I really learned a lot.
Some fools think of happiness
Some fools think of happiness
blissfulness, togetherness.
blissfulness, togetherness.
Some fools fool themselves, I guess.
Some fools fool themselves, I guess.
But they're not fooling me.
But they're not fooling me.

)))))))))))))))

In 1914, a sixteen-year-old Italian boy arrived at Ellis Island.

In 1914, a sixteen-year-old Italian boy arrived at Ellis Island.

He soon found a job in the kitchen at the Ritz Carlton, where he eventually worked his way up to Head Chef.

He soon found a job in the kitchen at the Ritz Carlton, where he eventually worked his way up to Head Chef.

During the first years of the Napoleonic Wars, the French government offered a hefty cash award to any inventor who could devise a cheap and effective method of preserving large amounts of food.

During the first years of the Napoleonic Wars, the French government offered a hefty cash award to any inventor who could devise a cheap and effective method of preserving large amounts of food.

Sixteen ounces of hamburger meat can contain meat and fat from 200-400 cattle from multiple states and two to four countries.

Sixteen ounces of hamburger meat can contain meat and fat from 200-400 cattle from multiple states and two to four countries.

Your daily mealtime tasks may seem unimportant, but when you serve foods that build strength and endurance and courage, you're helping to build victory.

Your daily mealtime tasks may seem unimportant, but when you serve foods that build strength and endurance and courage, you're helping to build victory.

Ettore Boiardi's likeness appears on ConAgra's Chef Boyardee canned pastas.

Ettore Boiardi's likeness appears on ConAgra's Chef Boyardee canned pastas.

Boiardi's last TV commercial aired in 1979.

Boiardi's last TV commercial aired in 1979.

In 2000 BC, people in what is now China ate noodles made of millet.

In 2000 BC, people in what is now China ate noodles made of millet.

ConAgra's products are available in supermarkets, as well as restaurants and food service establishments.

ConAgra's products are available in supermarkets, as well as restaurants and food service establishments.

In 1809, a French confectioner and brewer observed that food cooked inside a jar did not spoil unless the seals leaked.

In 1809, a French confectioner and brewer observed that food cooked inside a jar did not spoil unless the seals leaked.

A 4000-year-old bowl of millet noodles was discovered in Qinghai province, near Xi'ning Prison.

A 4000-year-old bowl of millet noodles was discovered in Qinghai province, near Xi'ning Prison.

Qinghai, which lies outside of China proper, has been an ethnic melting pot for centuries, mixing Tibetan, Han Chinese, Mongol, and Turkish influences.

Qinghai, which lies outside of China proper, has been an ethnic melting pot for centuries, mixing Tibetan, Han Chinese, Mongol, and Turkish influences.

In 1917, the Italian Army experimented with tinned ravioli and spaghetti bolognese.

In 1917, the Italian Army experimented with tinned ravioli and spaghetti bolognese.

The original Chef Boyardee dinner for four cost 60 cents.

The original Chef Boyardee dinner for four cost 60 cents.

It included uncooked spaghetti, sauce, and Parmesan cheese.

It included uncooked spaghetti, sauce, and Parmesan cheese.

Ettore Boiardi's likeness appears on ConAgra's Chef Boyardee canned pastas.

Ettore Boiardi's likeness appears on ConAgra's Chef Boyardee canned pastas.

In the late 1980s, Parma, Ohio, a suburb of Cleveland, suffered major financial problems.

In the late 1980s, Parma, Ohio, a suburb of Cleveland, suffered major financial problems.

Durum wheat pasta was introduced to Italy by Arabs during their conquest of Sicily in the late 7th century.

Durum wheat pasta was introduced to Italy by Arabs during their conquest of Sicily in the late 7th century.

In 1971, Consolidated Mills changed its name to ConAgra, a combination of con for consolidated and agra for from the earth in Latin. ConAgra is headquartered in Omaha, Nebraska.

In 1971, Consolidated Mills changed its name to ConAgra, a combination of *con* for consolidated and *agra* for from the earth in Latin. ConAgra is headquartered in Omaha, Nebraska.

For thousands of years, bison moved in expansive herds across what is now Cleveland and Omaha, eating the grasses down as they traveled to new grazing areas, leaving natural fertilizer—bodily waste and plant litter—in their wake.

For thousands of years, bison moved in expansive herds across what is now Cleveland and Omaha, eating the grasses down as they traveled to new grazing areas, leaving natural fertilizer—bodily waste and plant litter—in their wake.

This natural process helped to build the rich and fertile soils of the Midwest.

This natural process helped to build the rich and fertile soils of the Midwest.

Every soldier of food shares responsibility for supplying bodily ammunition to the unsung heroes who produce America's war weapons.

Every soldier of food shares responsibility for supplying bodily ammunition to the unsung heroes who produce America's war weapons.

In 1919, Boiardi moved to Cleveland to become Head Chef at the Hotel Winton.

In 1919, Boiardi moved to Cleveland to become Head Chef at the Hotel Winton.

In 2009, ConAgra brands was found in 97% percent of U.S. households.

In 2009, ConAgra brands was found in 97% percent of U.S. households.

Marco Polo did not import pasta from China.

Marco Polo did not import pasta from China.

Durum wheat was not known in China until later times.

Durum wheat was not known in China until later times.

In the 1840s, tinned food became a status symbol amongst middle-class households in Europe.

In the 1840s, tinned food became a status symbol amongst middle-class households in Europe.

Parma, Ohio, was once home to major industries, such as General Motors, Modern Tool & Die, the Union Carbide Research Center, and Cox Cable Television.

Parma, Ohio, was once home to major industries, such as General Motors, Modern Tool & Die, the Union Carbide Research Center, and Cox Cable Television.

Its tremendous growth came after World War II.

Its tremendous growth came after World War II.

The Food Front serves the fighting front and the home front.

The Food Front serves the fighting front and the home front.

From farmer to food worker to grocer to homemaker stretches the food front—the army behind the armies.

From farmer to food worker to grocer to homemaker stretches the food front—the army behind the armies.

In 1924, Boiardi opened his first restaurant, Giardino d' Italia, in

Cleveland.

In 1924, Boiardi opened his first restaurant, Giardino d' Italia, in Cleveland.

A special kitchen on the second floor filled takeout orders.

A special kitchen on the second floor filled takeout orders.

Large-scale wars in the nineteenth century provided canning companies with many opportunities for expansion.

Large-scale wars in the nineteenth century provided canning companies with many opportunities for expansion.

Demand for canned food skyrocketed during World War I.

Demand for canned food skyrocketed during World War I.

A great deal of what used to be Central American rainforest is now land cleared for raising cattle.

A great deal of what used to be Central American rainforest is now land cleared for raising cattle.

Urban populations demanded ever-increasing quantities of cheap, quality food that they could keep at home without having to go shopping daily.

Urban populations demanded ever-increasing quantities of cheap, quality food that they could keep at home without having to go shopping daily.

During World War II, Boiardi developed field rations for the armed services, providing millions of rations for American and Allied troops.

During World War II, Boiardi developed field rations for the armed services, providing millions of rations for American and Allied troops.

In the 1950s, 60s, and 70s, Consolidated Mills expanded its livestock feed business.

In the 1950s, 60s, and 70s, Consolidated Mills expanded its livestock feed business.

Napoleon put it this way: *An army marches on its stomach.*

Napoleon put it this way: *An army marches on its stomach.*

In 1945, Boiardi sold his business to American Home Foods for six million dollars.

In 1945, Boiardi sold his business to American Home Foods for six million dollars.

In 1985, Chef Boyardee brands grossed $500 million.

In 1985, Chef Boyardee brands grossed $500 million.

Durum wheat semolina with high gluten content is what makes pasta dough malleable.

Durum wheat semolina with high gluten content is what makes pasta dough malleable.

Well-managed cattle can greatly enhance the growth and propagation of grasses.

Well-managed cattle can greatly enhance the growth and propagation of grasses.

These grasses can sequester huge amounts of carbon annually.

These grasses can sequester huge amounts of carbon annually.

In the 1970s, as commodity speculation wiped out its margins on raw foods, ConAgra moved into the frozen food and packaged meat industries.

In the 1970s, as commodity speculation wiped out its margins on raw foods, ConAgra moved into the frozen food and packaged meat industries.

In 1946, Boiardi invested in steel mills—these steel mills helped produce goods needed for the Korean War.

In 1946, Boiardi invested in steel mills—these steel mills helped produce goods needed for the Korean War.

In 1985, Boiardi died in Parma, Ohio.

In 1985, Boiardi died in Parma, Ohio.

He used good pure beef, the kind you'd ask for at the butcher's.

He used good pure beef, the kind you'd ask for at the butcher's.

Beefaroni was delicious and nutritious, because the quick pep of macaroni was made more lasting by all the beefy protein.

Beefaroni was delicious and nutritious, because the quick pep of macaroni was made more lasting by all the beefy protein.

Children loved it, and company did too—it's hard to believe it cost only fourteen cents a serving.

Children loved it, and company did too—it's hard to believe it cost only fourteen cents a serving.

Canned goods sell especially well in times of recession due to cocooning, a term used by retail analysts to describe the phenomenon in which people actively avoid straying from their houses.

Canned goods sell especially well in times of recession due to cocooning, a term used by retail analysts to describe the phenomenon in which people actively avoid straying from their houses.

When victory comes it will not be the result of great battles alone, it will be a victory that began months or even years before, on farms, in food plants, and in your own kitchen.

When victory comes it will not be the result of great battles alone, it will be a victory that began months or even years before, on farms, in food plants, and in your own kitchen.

)))))))))))))))

O democracy.
O democracy.
You keep being this and not that.
You keep being this and not that.
I don't know what I want from you.
I don't know what I want from you.
You keep refusing to let me look at you, talk to you.
You keep refusing to let me look at you, talk to you.
I don't know what I want from you anymore.
I don't know what I want from you anymore.
You keep showing me nothing rather than something.
You keep showing me nothing rather than something.
You keep not signifying anything other than myself.
You keep not signifying anything other than myself.
I suppose I just don't know what I want from you.
I suppose I just don't know what I want from you.
Maybe I want you to grow out of our power plugs, or from the corners of our walls and ceilings.
Maybe I want you to grow out of our power plugs, or from the corners of our walls and ceilings.
Maybe I want you to stare holes into our books.
Maybe I want you to stare holes into our books.
Or into our chairs and tables.
Or into our chairs and tables.
Maybe I just want you to be a line that follows everywhere that my eye goes.
Maybe I just want you to be a line that follows everywhere that my eye goes.
Why don't you just tell me what I want?
Why don't you just tell me what I want?

You might have heard of Gideon's trumpet.
You might have heard of Gideon's trumpet.
Maybe you know he had a lot of them.
Maybe you know he had a lot of them.
You might also remember how an angel cooked his food
You might also remember how an angel cooked his food
by making fire come out of a rock
by making fire come out of a rock
or how Gideon tested God on His ability to control the morning
dew.
or how Gideon tested God on His ability to control the morning
dew.
Well, God arranged for Gideon to form an army
Well, God arranged for Gideon to form an army
and once Gideon's army had wiped the Midians off the map
and once Gideon's army had wiped the Midians off the map
his people said to him, *Gideon!*
his people said to him, *Gideon!*
You have delivered us from the Midians.
You have delivered us from the Midians.
Rule over us!
Rule over us!
But Gideon said, *No, I will not rule over you.*
But Gideon said, *No, I will not rule over you.*
The Lord will do that.
The Lord will do that.
However I do have one small request.
However I do have one small request.
I want you to give me the earrings
I want you to give me the earrings
of all the men you killed.
of all the men you killed.
So the men of Israel got together
So the men of Israel got together
and spread a cloth on the ground
and spread a cloth on the ground
and threw down all the earrings they had collected
and threw down all the earrings they had collected
as well as a bunch of ornaments
as well as a bunch of ornaments
and collars and chains and stuff
and collars and chains and stuff
and Gideon had it all melted down
and Gideon had it all melted down
and made into an ephod.

and made into an ephod.

When Gideon put this ephod in his city

When Gideon put this ephod in his city

all Israel went thither a whoring after it.

all Israel went thither a whoring after it.

This ephod thing, we're told

This ephod thing, we're told

soon became a snare

soon became a snare

unto Gideon and to his house.

unto Gideon and to his house.

So what is an ephod?

So what is an ephod?

According to Wikipedia

According to Wikipedia

many experts believe *ephod*

many experts believe *ephod*

denotes an oracular image encased in gold.

denotes an oracular image encased in gold.

Whatever that means.

Whatever that means.

It was something to go thither a whoring after

It was something to go thither a whoring after

we know that much.

we know that much.

A bad idea, that's for sure.

A bad idea, that's for sure.

)))))))))))))))

O dragon.
O dragon.
Be positive.
Be positive.
Consider lifestyle.
Consider lifestyle.
Consider becoming.
Consider becoming.
Eventuality.
Eventuality.
Consequences.
Consequences.
Talk to your therapist.
Talk to your therapist.
Get to *dragon*
Get to *dragon*
or another name
or another name
with some psychological economy.
with some psychological economy.
Don't worry about legitimating certain moves.
Don't worry about legitimating certain moves.
Go ahead and become a subjective subject
Go ahead and become a subjective subject
and not a description
and not a description
or a critique
or a critique
or a deconstruction.
or a deconstruction.
Get to *becoming.*
Get to *becoming.*
Becoming—eventuality—enables us to consider consequences
in a particular way.
**Becoming—eventuality—enables us to consider consequences
in a particular way.**
Get to *consequences.*
Get to *consequences.*
Get to the Forbidden City.
Get to the Forbidden City.
Notice all the dragons

Notice all the dragons
on roofs and doors
on roofs and doors
pillars and bridges.
pillars and bridges.
Utensils.
Utensils.
Buy a yellow robe covered in five-clawed dragons.
Buy a yellow robe covered in five-clawed dragons.
Don't leave the Forbidden City without a yellow robe
Don't leave the Forbidden City without a yellow robe
covered in five-clawed dragons.
covered in five-clawed dragons.
Wear your yellow robe covered in five-clawed dragons.
Wear your yellow robe covered in five-clawed dragons.
Be misty
Be misty
mystic
mystic
occulted
occulted
noble
noble
untouchable
untouchable
and free of guarantees
and free of guarantees
or systems.
or systems.

)))))))))))))))

Better clear your history, honey.
Better clear your history, honey.
Better clear your cache.
Better clear your cache.
We did the non-disclosure agreement
We did the non-disclosure agreement
so ya know that
so ya know that
No person shall access classified material on the web
No person shall access classified material on the web
as doin so risks material still classified being placed onto non-classified systems.
as doin so risks material still classified being placed onto non-classified systems.
We did that trainin on the proper safeguardin of classified information
We did that trainin on the proper safeguardin of classified information
so ya know that
so ya know that
No person shall access classified material on the web
No person shall access classified material on the web
unless a favorable determination of the person's eligibility for access
unless a favorable determination of the person's eligibility for access
has been made by an agency head.
has been made by an agency head.
We did the session on criminal, civil, and administrative sanctions
We did the session on criminal, civil, and administrative sanctions
so ya know that
so ya know that
except as authorized by their agencies
except as authorized by their agencies
and pursuant to agency procedures
and pursuant to agency procedures
means somethin.
means somethin.
Better clear your downloads, darlin.
Better clear your downloads, darlin.
Clear your temporary files.

Clear your temporary files.

Then look me in the eye, babe
Then look me in the eye, babe
and see a night sky full of stars.
and see a night sky full of stars.
Ya know
Ya know
everythin's gon be alright.
everythin's gon be alright.

)))))))))))))))

Don't call this little guy a teddy bear.
Don't call this little guy a teddy bear.

He's a police bear.
He's a police bear.

Teddy bears don't wear blue button-down shirts and black pants and ties and shiny black shoes.
Teddy bears don't wear blue button-down shirts and black pants and ties and shiny black shoes.

Teddy bears don't wear a police hat and badge and belt with a holster and gun.
Teddy bears don't wear a police hat and badge and belt with a holster and gun.

When off-duty he maintains a search pattern for every violation he could ticket if on duty.
When off-duty he maintains a search pattern for every violation he could ticket if on duty.

Don't be fooled by the blank expression. He's gathering information. He studying every single little girl in this crowd.
Don't be fooled by the blank expression. He's gathering information. He studying every single little girl in this crowd.

He's taking note of physical details and measurements, such as eye color, eyebrow shape, hair color, hairstyle, clothing, body-type.
He's taking note of physical details and measurements, such as eye color, eyebrow shape, hair color, hairstyle, clothing, body-type.

Being trained to read expressions and body language, he's observant and intuitive, which makes him very pleasant company.
Being trained to read expressions and body language, he's observant and intuitive, which makes him very pleasant company.

He knows the little girls who pick him up have a present and a past, and he's not afraid to ask them questions.
He knows the little girls who pick him up have a present and a past, and he's not afraid to ask them questions.

He steers right toward the hard stuff and doesn't flinch if they don't want to admit certain things.
He steers right toward the hard stuff and doesn't flinch if they don't want to admit certain things.

That's the great thing about his job.
That's the great thing about his job.

The crimes little girls commit can hardly be called crimes.
The crimes little girls commit can hardly be called crimes.

The police bear sees generalizations as being important to efficient functioning.

The police bear sees generalizations as being important to efficient functioning.

Though he's willing to acknowledge exceptions, he finds that men, women, gang-bangers, Mexicans, yuppies, gays, even police bears, do have certain tendencies, so he doesn't see any problem stating what those are.

Though he's willing to acknowledge exceptions, he finds that men, women, gang-bangers, Mexicans, yuppies, gays, even police bears, do have certain tendencies, so he doesn't see any problem stating what those are.

For example, *Police bears crave authority and honey*.

For example, *Police bears crave authority and honey*.

)))))))))))))))

How do I know Cæsar was stabbed twenty-three times?
How do I know Cæsar was stabbed twenty-three times?
Not nineteen, not thirty-six, but twenty-three.
Not nineteen, not thirty-six, but twenty-three.
Maybe you're wondering how I know Julius Cæsar even existed.
Maybe you're wondering how I know Julius Cæsar even existed.
How do I know it was Washington, not Rochambeau, who won the
Revolutionary War?
How do I know it was Washington, not Rochambeau, who won the
Revolutionary War?
By having it on good authority.
By having it on good authority.
Municipal officials are looting the city treasury.
Municipal officials are looting the city treasury.
German spies are spreading the boll-weevil through the South
German spies are spreading the boll-weevil through the South
by casting the insect from moving trains.
by casting the insect from moving trains.
Secret agents of the Pope are infiltrating the Bureau of Engraving
Secret agents of the Pope are infiltrating the Bureau of Engraving
to introduce pictures of His Holiness
to introduce pictures of His Holiness
among the decorations on the dollar bill.
among the decorations on the dollar bill.
The Battle of San Juan Hill will be a terrible fight.
The Battle of San Juan Hill will be a terrible fight.

)))))))))))))))

O videogame.
O videogame.
We're just bursting with criminal potential.
We're just bursting with criminal potential.
We can imagine ourselves committing any crime.
We can imagine ourselves committing any crime.
But we need you to help us imagine.
But we need you to help us imagine.
We need you to disturb the equilibrium of our social instincts.
We need you to disturb the equilibrium of our social instincts.
And to repeat the process.
And to repeat the process.
Only by force of repetition can our dark souls become accustomed to their reflections.
Only by force of repetition can our dark souls become accustomed to their reflections.
We need you to awake those criminal memories that lay sleeping in our blood.
We need you to awake those criminal memories that lay sleeping in our blood.
Only by force of repetition can these memories be purged.
Only by force of repetition can these memories be purged.
Nothing's more moral in effect than your immorality.
Nothing's more moral in effect than your immorality.
Endow us with the power of self-control.
Endow us with the power of self-control.
Enable us to experience error and catastrophe with zero personal cost.
Enable us to experience error and catastrophe with zero personal cost.
We need your simulated circumstances to prepare us for remorse.
We need your simulated circumstances to prepare us for remorse.

)))))))))))))))

Not one lawyer on *Law & Order*

Not one lawyer on *Law & Order*

has Zuzu's petals in his or her pocket.

has Zuzu's petals in his or her pocket.

If you've never worked professionally and aren't sure how professionals dress then just look at these *Law & Order* lawyers.

If you've never worked professionally and aren't sure how professionals dress then just look at these *Law & Order* lawyers.

Their suits are well tailored, and have no loose threads or pills.

Their suits are well tailored, and have no loose threads or pills.

They're always gray, charcoal, or very dark blue.

They're always gray, charcoal, or very dark blue.

Suits!

Suits!

You won't find anyone in the D.A.'s office on *Law & Order* wearing a sport coat and slacks.

You won't find anyone in the D.A.'s office on *Law & Order* wearing a sport coat and slacks.

And look in their pockets.

And look in their pockets.

Zuzu's petals aren't in them.

Zuzu's petals aren't in them.

People say, *This is America.*

People say, *This is America.*

We should be able to do what we want.

We should be able to do what we want.

But rights and freedoms are regulated.

But rights and freedoms are regulated.

Courthouse guards have the legal authority to examine anything you're carrying

Courthouse guards have the legal authority to examine anything you're carrying

whether you're carrying it in a briefcase, or on your person.

whether you're carrying it in a briefcase, or on your person.

Dress codes are protected by law.

Dress codes are protected by law.

)))))))))))))))

WHAT IS TO BE DONE STOP
WHAT IS TO BE DONE STOP
FOUNDATIONS OF FREE SOCIETY UNDER ATTACK STOP
FOUNDATIONS OF FREE SOCIETY UNDER ATTACK STOP
YOUNG PEOPLE CONDEMN MORE THAN COMMEND STOP
YOUNG PEOPLE CONDEMN MORE THAN COMMEND STOP
ASSAULT ON FREE ENTERPRISE GAINING MOMENTUM STOP
ASSAULT ON FREE ENTERPRISE GAINING MOMENTUM STOP
PUBLIC CONFIDENCE BEING UNDERMINED STOP
PUBLIC CONFIDENCE BEING UNDERMINED STOP
WORKERS BEING PITTED AGAINST MANAGEMENT STOP
WORKERS BEING PITTED AGAINST MANAGEMENT STOP
OBJECTIVE OF CRITICS TO CONFUSE AMERICAN PUBLIC STOP
OBJECTIVE OF CRITICS TO CONFUSE AMERICAN PUBLIC STOP
YOUNG PEOPLE LIVING BY MINDLESS SLOGANS STOP
YOUNG PEOPLE LIVING BY MINDLESS SLOGANS STOP
HIGH TIME WE EXERCISE OUR POLITICAL INFLUENCE STOP
HIGH TIME WE EXERCISE OUR POLITICAL INFLUENCE STOP
SURVIVAL OF AMERICAN SYSTEM AT STAKE STOP
SURVIVAL OF AMERICAN SYSTEM AT STAKE STOP
BUSINESSMEN MUST THINK ABOUT MORE THAN PROFIT STOP
BUSINESSMEN MUST THINK ABOUT MORE THAN PROFIT STOP
YOUNG PEOPLE DESPISE THE ECONOMIC SYSTEM STOP
YOUNG PEOPLE DESPISE THE ECONOMIC SYSTEM STOP
MUST PROMOTE GENUINE UNDERSTANDING OF SYSTEM STOP
MUST PROMOTE GENUINE UNDERSTANDING OF SYSTEM STOP

)))))))))))))))

If someone picks up the check
If someone picks up the check
send them an e-mail right away, thanking them.
send them an e-mail right away, thanking them.
Tell them how much you enjoyed the meal and the conversation.
Tell them how much you enjoyed the meal and the conversation.
If you meet someone at a party who tells a funny story then send them an e-mail about how you were still chuckling over it on the way home.
If you meet someone at a party who tells a funny story then send them an e-mail about how you were still chuckling over it on the way home.
Secretaries are very often neglected.
Secretaries are very often neglected.
Every once in a while you might send your wife's secretary an e-mail to let her know how much you appreciate all of the little things she does for the Missus.
Every once in a while you might send your wife's secretary an e-mail to let her know how much you appreciate all of the little things she does for the Missus.
Elderly people are more likely than most to be forgotten or ignored.
Elderly people are more likely than most to be forgotten or ignored.
Try sending them an e-mail.
Try sending them an e-mail.
Let them know that you care about them
Let them know that you care about them
and that they haven't been forgotten after all.
and that they haven't been forgotten after all.

)))))))))))))))

It's Green Beret party time again.
It's Green Beret party time again.
Green Berets drinking and laughing and singing:
Green Berets drinking and laughing and singing:
Joy to the warriors!
Joy to the warriors!
Joy to the victors!
Joy to the victors!
Peace to our brethren that fell in the fray!
Peace to our brethren that fell in the fray!
We're victorious in war!
We're victorious in war!
We're generous in peace!
We're generous in peace!
We're the true followers of Kennedy!
We're the true followers of Kennedy!
Of Nixon!
Of Nixon!
Of Ford!
Of Ford!
Of Carter!
Of Carter!
Of Reagan!
Of Reagan!
Of Bush!
Of Bush!
Of Clinton!
Of Clinton!
Of Bush!
Of Bush!
Of Obama!
Of Obama!

)))))))))))))))

The needle's eye
The needle's eye
Jesus spoke of
Jesus spoke of
was actually a place
was actually a place
called Needle's Eye.
called Needle's Eye.
It was a mountain passage
It was a mountain passage
on a major trade route
on a major trade route
that was extremely narrow.
that was extremely narrow.
So narrow that camels
So narrow that camels
loaded down with goods
loaded down with goods
could not pass through.
could not pass through.
Basically you had to unload everything
Basically you had to unload everything
and carry it all
and carry it all
through the narrow passage
through the narrow passage
piece by piece
piece by piece
and then load up your camels again
and then load up your camels again
on the other side
on the other side
so it was very difficult
so it was very difficult
but not impossible.
but not impossible.

)))))))))))))))

Twin beds are back.
Twin beds are back.
Want to make your bed?
Want to make your bed?
Fine.
Fine.
Don't want to make your bed?
Don't want to make your bed?
Fine.
Fine.
What's the greatest His-and-Hers invention of all time?
What's the greatest His-and-Hers invention of all time?
TWIN BEDS.
TWIN BEDS.
Want silk sheets?
Want silk sheets?
Fine.
Fine.
Cotton?
Cotton?
Go ahead.
Go ahead.
A bunch of pillows?
A bunch of pillows?
Fine.
Fine.
No pillows?
No pillows?
Fine.
Fine.
Convenience, comfort.
Convenience, comfort.
Toss and turn all you want.
Toss and turn all you want.
TWIN BEDS, baby. What are we waiting for?
TWIN BEDS, baby. What are we waiting for?

)))))))))))))))

Saint Valentine!
Saint Valentine!
Martyred by being clubbed to death and afterwards beheaded
Martyred by being clubbed to death and afterwards beheaded
Fourteen February in the Year of Our Lord 269.
Fourteen February in the Year of Our Lord 269.
The fourteenth had long been associated with the mating of birds, and as a result his name was given to human courting missives.
The fourteenth had long been associated with the mating of birds, and as a result his name was given to human courting missives.
Valentines!
Valentines!
This custom is said to have pagan antecedents connected with the worship of Juno.
This custom is said to have pagan antecedents connected with the worship of Juno.
Jupiter's wife!
Jupiter's wife!
Valentines sent by the hopeful of either sex to the desired one achieved immense popularity in Victorian times.
Valentines sent by the hopeful of either sex to the desired one achieved immense popularity in Victorian times.
Queen Victoria!
Queen Victoria!
In recent years, the use of valentines has been revived, though on more humorous and less saccharine lines.
In recent years, the use of valentines has been revived, though on more humorous and less saccharine lines.
Valentines can be purchased at Woolworth's by the hopeful of either sex for five cents.
Valentines can be purchased at Woolworth's by the hopeful of either sex for five cents.
Franklin Woolworth!
Franklin Woolworth!

)))))))))))))))

What is badness?
What is badness?
That which often
That which often
thou hast already seen
thou hast already seen
and known.
and known.
O ye men and women
O ye men and women
of Manhattan
of Manhattan
look above and below
look above and below
and thou shalt find
and thou shalt find
but the same things.
but the same things.
Stand on the sidewalk
Stand on the sidewalk
and look up
and look up
at the slice of gray sky
at the slice of gray sky
or stand by the window
or stand by the window
and look down
and look down
at rows of yellow cabs
at rows of yellow cabs
or look back
or look back
upon things of former ages
upon things of former ages
the manifold changes
the manifold changes
of monarchies
of monarchies
and commonwealths
and commonwealths
and what does thou see

and what does thou see
but the very same things
but the very same things
whereof ancient stories
whereof ancient stories
and *New York Times* stories
and *New York Times* stories
and *Wall Street Journal* stories
and *Wall Street Journal* stories
and *New York Post* stories
and *New York Post* stories
are full
are full
and whereof shopping malls
and whereof shopping malls
are full
are full
and gyms
and gyms
are full
are full
and mailboxes
and mailboxes
are full.
are full.
Bad views
Bad views
bad wishes
bad wishes
bad designs.
bad designs.
There is nothing that is new.
There is nothing that is new.
The things of the world
The things of the world
good and bad
good and bad
thou hast already seen them.
thou hast already seen them.
Pizza slices for truant teens
Pizza slices for truant teens
wires for little puppets
wires for little puppets

holes for terrified mice
holes for terrified mice
signs for peaceful protestors
signs for peaceful protestors
bones for hungry dogs
bones for hungry dogs
plastic shields for riot police
plastic shields for riot police
chum for sleepless sharks
chum for sleepless sharks
these be the objects of the world
these be the objects of the world
good things and bad things
good things and bad things
the worth of which
the worth of which
ye men and women of Manhattan
ye men and women of Manhattan
thou doth affect in every deed.
thou doth affect in every deed.
O reasonable creatures
O reasonable creatures
thou are ordained
thou are ordained
one for another
one for another
and being ordained thus
and being ordained thus
what is chief in thine own constitution
what is chief in thine own constitution
is the intent to pursue the common good.
is the intent to pursue the common good.
Therefore whensoever thou doth trespass
Therefore whensoever thou doth trespass
against thine own fellow Americans
against thine own fellow Americans
I will do my damnedest to consider
I will do my damnedest to consider
what it was
what it was
that thou did suppose to be bad
that thou did suppose to be bad
and what it was

and what it was
that thou did suppose to be good
that thou did suppose to be good
when thou did trespass.
when thou did trespass.
so that I might pity thee
so that I may pity thee
and have no occasion
and have no occasion
either to wonder
either to wonder
or be angry.
or be angry.

)))))))))))))))

O whales.
O whales.
I read in the paper that you tried communism
I read in the paper that you tried communism
and it didn't work.
and it didn't work.
That you'd tried it fifty million years ago
That you'd tried it fifty million years ago
by going to live in the sea.
by going to live in the sea.
Because you couldn't take anything with you.
Because you couldn't take anything with you.
Just your mammal selves.
Just your mammal selves.
Just each other.
Just each other.
Since there was plenty of food in the sea
Since there was plenty of food in the sea
you didn't have to worry about foraging
you didn't have to worry about foraging
or hunting
or hunting
or competing for territory.
or competing for territory.
No worries about food or shelter or clothing.
No worries about food or shelter or clothing.
No one had to make anything of themselves
No one had to make anything of themselves
because there was no basis for individual achievement.
because there was no basis for individual achievement.
No one got stuck being a bellhop.
No one got stuck being a bellhop.
Or a vice president.
Or a vice president.
The employment rate was one hundred percent.
The employment rate was one hundred percent.
The unemployment rate was one hundred percent.
The unemployment rate was one hundred percent.
You've spent your lives
You've spent your lives
trying to be good husbands

trying to be good husbands
and wives
and wives
good fathers
good fathers
and sons
and sons
good mothers
good mothers
and daughters
and daughters
good brothers
good brothers
and sisters
and sisters
good grandparents
good grandparents
and grandchildren
and grandchildren
good uncles
good uncles
and aunts
and aunts
good cousins
good cousins
and friends.
and friends.

)))))))))))))))

Let us look back on History pages, if you please.

Let us look back on History pages, if you please.

Thirty years ago our Great City lay in a Bed of Ashes.

Thirty years ago our Great City lay in a Bed of Ashes.

But will you look at her today?

But will you look at her today?

Look where she stands.

Look where she stands.

Look how far we have flown on the Wings of Prosperity.

Look how far we have flown on the Wings of Prosperity.

She has risen, Gentlemen, she has risen.

She has risen, Gentlemen, she has risen.

From a Bed of Destruction she has risen.

From a Bed of Destruction she has risen.

Today she is pronounced the Queen City.

Today she is pronounced the Queen City.

Today she is pronounced the Jewel in the Crown.

Today she is pronounced the Jewel in the Crown.

Who brought us this Progress? Who lifted her up?

Who brought us this Progress? Who lifted her up?

Who cast off the Robes of Destruction?

Who cast off the Robes of Destruction?

Who wrapped her in the Loyal Garments she wears today?

Who wrapped her in the Loyal Garments she wears today?

Was it the People? No.

Was it the People? No.

It was you, Gentlemen. It was you.

It was you, Gentlemen. It was you.

What Gallantry you displayed! What Fierce Commitment!

What Gallantry you displayed! What Fierce Commitment!

Inspired by your Duty, we endured.

Inspired by your Duty, we endured.

Inspired by your Wisdom, we prevailed.

Inspired by your Wisdom, we prevailed.

Look at all your Manhood has secured.

Look at all your Manhood has secured.

))))))))))))))))

Occupy!
Occupy!
What spectacle and virtuosity!
What spectacle and virtuosity!
What transformation and magic
What transformation and magic
and make-believe!
and make-believe!
Your glamour
Your glamour
and transcendency of the star image
and transcendency of the star image
the heroic
the heroic
and anti-heroic
and anti-heroic
your trash imagery
your trash imagery
and involvement of performers
and involvement of performers
and spectators
and spectators
your style
your style
and camp
and camp
and camping
and camping
and the seduction of spectators
and the seduction of spectators
by the wiles of your performers
by the wiles of your performers
and your eccentricities
and your eccentricities
your moving
your moving
and being moved
and being moved
well what can we say?
well what can we say?
Wow.

Wow.
But now...

But now...

has something gone wrong?

has something gone wrong?

Are you moon-struck?

Are you moon-struck?

Or was something wrong all along?

Or was something wrong all along?

What shall we do?

What shall we do?

What ought we to do?

What ought we to do?

Rid ourselves of you, we must.

Rid ourselves of you, we must.

Go, you shall.

Go, you shall.

One of two things must take place:

One of two things must take place:

either you must do something

either you must do something

or something

or something

must be done to you.

must be done to you.

O Occupy. O humanity.

O Occupy. O humanity.

ACKNOWLEDGEMENTS

"A Basic Requirement of Modern Life," "Boiardi" and "Train Station" (alternate versions) previously appeared in *Mad Hatters' Review*. "Cop About to Give Himself a Ticket" and "Teenagers with Glocks" (alternate versions) previously appeared in *DIAGRAM*. "Proletarian Television Producers" and "The Time Is Now" (alternate versions) previously appeared in *Pacific Review*. "Twin Beds Are Back" (alternate version) previously appeared in *Barely South*.

CREDITS

Mark Aguhar ◊ Muhammad Ali ◊ Marcus Aurelius ◊ Bob Avakian
Charles Baudelaire ◊ Jean Baudrillard ◊ Charles Bernstein
Gwendolyn Brooks ◊ Felice Bryant ◊ Jane Fonda ◊ Michel Foucault
Sigmund Freud ◊ Tiffany Funk ◊ Allen Ginsberg ◊ Barry Goldwater
Antonio Gramsci ◊ Eric Hobsbawm ◊ Emma Lazarus
Richard Lemon ◊ Jack London ◊ Deirdre McCloskey
Herman Melville ◊ C. Wright Mills ◊ Edmund H. North
Claes Oldenburg ◊ Lewis Powell ◊ Yvonne Rainer
Laurie Jo Reynolds ◊ Karl Rove ◊ J.D. Salinger ◊ Sir Walter Scott
Valerie Solanas ◊ John Steinbeck ◊ Joe Strummer ◊ Tina Tahir
Henry David Thoreau ◊ Donald Trump ◊ Walt Whitman
Oscar Wilde

THANKS

Mark Aguhar ◊ Rae Armantrout ◊ Jennifer Ashton ◊ Ian Curry
Lennard Davis ◊ Ben Doller ◊ Sandra Doller ◊ Tiffany Funk
LeeAnn Lodder ◊ Kera MacKenzie ◊ Anthony Madrid
Donato Mancini ◊ Mike McFarland ◊ Sparkle McFarland
Carrie Messenger ◊ Chris Messenger ◊ Walter Benn Michaels
James Pate ◊ Raúl Peña ◊ Alex Rauch ◊ Jennifer Reeder
Matthias Regan ◊ Gladys Reynolds ◊ Pud Reynolds
Davis Schneiderman ◊ Daniel Shea ◊ Tina Tahir ◊ Luis Urrea
Gene Wildman

More titles from 1913 Press:

Full Moon Hawk Application, CA Conrad (Assless Chaps, 2014)
Big House/Disclosure, Mendi & Keith Obadike (2013)
Four Electric Ghosts, Mendi & Keith Obadike (2013)
Kala Pani, Monica Mody (2013)
The Transfer Tree, Karena Youtz (2012)
Conversities, Dan Beachy-Quick & Srikanth Reddy (2012)
Home/Birth: A Poemic, Arielle Greenberg & Rachel Zucker (2011)
Wonderbender, Diane Wald (2011)
Ozalid, Biswamit Dwibedy (2010)
Sightings, Shin Yu Pai (2007)
Seismosis, John Keene & Christopher Stackhouse (2006)
Read 1-4 an anthology of inter-translation, Sarah Riggs & Cole Swensen, eds.
1913 a journal of forms, Issues 1-6

Forthcoming:

Abra, Amaranth Borsuk & Kate Durbin (2014)
Strong Suits, Brad Flis (2014)
Pomme & Granite, Sarah Riggs (2014)
Untimely Death is Driven Out Beyond the Horizon, Brenda Iijima (2014)
The Wrong Book, Nathaniel Otting (2015)
Hg-the liquid, Ward Tietz (2015)

1913 titles are distributed by Small Press Distribution
www.spdbooks.org
& printed on recycled papers.

Take a trip with me in 1913,
To Calumet, Michigan, in the copper country.
I will take you to a place called Italian Hall,
Where the miners are having their big Christmas ball.

WOODY GUTHRIE
1913 MASSACRE